Lean & Green Air Fryer Cookbook

Stay Healthy with These Delicious Recipes

Roxana Sutton

TABLE OF CONTENTS

Sweet and Spicy Air Fried Sweet Potatoes

Prep Time: 10 mins

Cook Time: 15 mins

Total Time: 25 mins

Ingredients

- 1 large sweet potato, cut into 1/2-inch pieces
- 1 tablespoon olive oil
- 1 tablespoon packed light brown sugar
- ¼ teaspoon sea salt
- ¼ teaspoon chili powder
- ¼ teaspoon ground paprika
- ¼ teaspoon cayenne pepper
- ⅛ teaspoon onion powder
- Ground black pepper to taste

Instructions

Preheat an air fryer to 400 degrees F (200 degrees C) according to the manufacturer's instructions. Place sweet potato in a large bowl. Drizzle with olive oil, then add brown sugar, salt, chili powder, paprika, cayenne pepper, onion powder, and pepper. Stir until potatoes are evenly coated and spread out onto the air fryer rack.

Cook on the upper rack of the preheated air fryer until browned and crispy, 15 to 20 minutes.

Nutrition Facts

Calories: 189; Protein 2.5g; Carbohydrates 35.3g; Fat 4.7g; Sodium 233.6mg.

Rosemary Potato Wedges For The Air Fryer

Prep Time: 10 mins

Cook Time: 20 mins

Total Time: 30 mins

Ingredients

- 2 russet potatoes, sliced into 12 wedges each with skin on
- 1 tablespoon extra-virgin olive oil
- 2 teaspoons seasoned salt
- 1 tablespoon finely chopped fresh rosemary

Instructions

Preheat an air fryer to 380 degrees F (190 degrees C).

Place potatoes in a large bowl and toss with olive oil. Sprinkle with seasoned salt and rosemary and toss to combine.

Place potatoes in an even layer in a fryer basket once the air fryer is hot; you may need to cook them in batches.

Air fry potatoes for 10 minutes, then flip wedges with tongs. Continue air frying until potato wedges reach the desired doneness, about 10 minutes more.

Nutrition Facts

Calories: 115; Protein 2.2g; Carbohydrates 19.2g; Fat 3.5g; Sodium 465.3mg.

Air Fryer Roasted Cauliflower

Prep Time: 10 mins

Cook Time: 15 mins

Total Time: 25 mins

Ingredients

- 3 cloves garlic
- 1 tablespoon peanut oil
- ½ teaspoon salt
- ½ teaspoon smoked paprika
- 4 cups cauliflower florets

Instructions

Preheat an air fryer to 400 degrees F (200 degrees C).

Cut garlic in half and smash with the blade of a knife. Place in a bowl with oil, salt, and paprika. Add cauliflower and turn to coat.

Place the coated cauliflower in the bowl of the air fryer and cook to desired crispiness, shaking every 5 minutes, about 15 minutes total.

Nutrition Facts

Calories: 118; Protein 4.3g; Carbohydrates 12.4g; Fat 7g; Sodium 642.3mg.

Air-Fried Ratatouille, Italian-Style

Prep Time: 25 mins

Cook Time: 25 mins

Additional Time: 5 mins

Total Time: 55 mins

Ingredients

- ½ small eggplant, cut into cubes
- 1 zucchini, cut into cubes
- 1 medium tomato, cut into cubes
- ½ large yellow bell pepper, cut into cubes
- ½ large red bell pepper, cut into cubes
- ½ onion, cut into cubes
- 1 fresh cayenne pepper, diced
- 5 sprigs fresh basil, stemmed and chopped
- 2 sprigs of fresh oregano, stemmed and chopped
- 1 clove garlic, crushed
- salt and ground black pepper to taste
- 1 tablespoon olive oil
- 1 tablespoon white wine

- 1 teaspoon vinegar

Instructions

Preheat an air fryer to 400 degrees F (200 degrees C).

Place eggplant, zucchini, tomato, bell peppers, and onion in a bowl. Add cayenne pepper, basil, oregano, garlic, salt, and pepper. Mix well to distribute everything evenly. Drizzle in oil, wine, and vinegar, mixing to coat all the vegetables.

Pour vegetable mixture into a baking dish and insert it into the basket of the air fryer. Cook for 8 minutes. Stir; cook for another 8 minutes. Stir again and continue cooking until tender, stirring every 5 minutes, 10 to 15 minutes more. Turn off the air fryer, leaving the dish inside. Let rest for 5 minutes before serving.

Nutritional Value

Calories: 79; Protein 2.1g; Carbohydrates 10.2g; Fat 3.8g; Sodium 47.6mg.

Air Fryer Spicy Green Beans

Prep Time: 10 mins

Cook Time: 25 mins

Additional Time: 5 mins

Total Time: 40 mins

Ingredients

- 12 ounces fresh green beans, trimmed
- 1 tablespoon sesame oil
- 1 teaspoon soy sauce
- 1 teaspoon rice wine vinegar
- 1 clove garlic, minced
- ½ teaspoon red pepper flakes

Instructions

Preheat an air fryer to 400 degrees F (200 degrees C).

Place green beans in a bowl. Whisk together sesame oil, soy sauce, rice wine vinegar, garlic, and red pepper flakes in a separate bowl and pour over green beans. Toss to coat and let marinate for 5 minutes. Place half the green beans in the air fryer basket. Cook 12 minutes, shaking the basket halfway through cooking time. Repeat with remaining green beans.

Nutrition Facts

Calories: 60; Protein 1.7g; Carbohydrates 6.6g; Fat 3.6g; Sodium 80mg.

Chinese Five-Spice Air Fryer Butternut Squash Fries

Prep Time: 15 mins

Cook Time: 15 mins

Total Time: 30 mins

Ingredients

- 1 large butternut squash, peeled and cut into "fries"
- 2 tablespoons olive oil
- 1 tablespoon Chinese five-spice powder
- 1 tablespoon minced garlic
- 2 teaspoons sea salt
- 2 teaspoons black pepper

Instructions

Preheat the air fryer to 400 degrees F (200 degrees C).

Place cut the squash in a large bowl. Add oil, five-spice powder, garlic, salt, and black pepper, and toss to coat.

Cook butternut squash fries in the preheated air fryer, shaking every 5 minutes, until crisp, 15 to 20 minutes total. Remove fries and season with additional sea salt.

Nutrition Facts

Calories: 150; Protein 2.5g; Carbohydrates 28.5g; Fat 4.9g; Sodium 596.4mg.

Air Fryer Brussels Sprouts

Prep Time: 5 mins

Cook Time: 10 mins

Total Time: 15 mins

Ingredients

- 1 teaspoon avocado oil
- ½ teaspoon salt
- ½ teaspoon ground black pepper
- 10 ounces Brussels sprouts, trimmed and halved lengthwise
- 1 teaspoon balsamic vinegar
- 2 teaspoons crumbled cooked bacon (optional)

Instructions

Preheat an air fryer to 350 degrees F (175 degrees C).

Combine oil, salt, and pepper in a bowl and mix well. Add Brussels sprouts and turn to coat. Air fry for 5 minutes, shake the sprouts and cook for an additional 5 minutes.

Transfer sprouts to a serving dish and sprinkles with balsamic vinegar; turn to coat. Sprinkle with bacon.

Nutrition Facts

Calories: 94; Protein 5.8g; Carbohydrates 13.3g; Fat 3.4g; Cholesterol 1.7mg; Sodium 690.6mg.

Air Fryer Root Vegetables With Vegan Aioli

Prep Time: 30 mins

Cook Time: 30 mins

Total Time: 1 hr

Ingredients

Garlic Aioli:

- ½ cup vegan mayonnaise (such as Vegenaise)
- 1 clove garlic, minced
- ½ teaspoon fresh lemon juice
- Salt and ground black pepper to taste

Root Vegetables:

- 4 tablespoons extra virgin olive oil
- 1 tablespoon minced fresh rosemary
- 3 cloves garlic, finely minced
- 1 teaspoon kosher salt, or to taste
- ½ teaspoon ground black pepper, or to taste
- 1 pound parsnips, peeled and cut vertically into uniform pieces

- 1 pound baby red potatoes, cut lengthwise into 4 or 6 pieces
- ½ pound baby carrots split lengthwise
- ½ red onion cut lengthwise into 1/2-inch slices
- ½ teaspoon grated lemon zest, or to taste (Optional)

Instructions

Combine mayonnaise, garlic, lemon juice, salt, and pepper in a small bowl for the garlic aioli; place in the refrigerator until ready to serve.

Preheat the air fryer to 400 degrees F (200 degrees C) if your air fryer manufacturer recommends preheating.

Combine olive oil, rosemary, garlic, salt, and pepper in a small bowl; set aside to allow the flavors to mingle. Combine parsnips, potatoes, carrots, and onion in a large bowl. Add olive oil-rosemary mixture and stir until vegetables are evenly coated. Place a portion of vegetables in a single layer in the basket of the air fryer, then add a rack and another layer of vegetables.

Air fry for 15 minutes.

When the timer sounds, you may plate the veggies and keep warm, or continue cooking in 5-minute intervals until the vegetables reach desired doneness and browning.

Place remaining vegetables in the bottom of the air fryer basket and air fry for 15 minutes, checking for doneness, as needed. Use the rack again, if you have more vegetables then fit in a single layer. When all the vegetables have cooked, serve with garlic aioli and garnish with lemon zest.

Nutrition Facts

calories; protein 2.2g; carbohydrates 25.5g; fat 13.8g; sodium 338.3mg.

Air Fryer Roasted Broccoli And Cauliflower

Prep Time: 10 mins

Cook Time: 15 mins

Total Time: 25 mins

Ingredients

- 3 cups broccoli florets
- 3 cups cauliflower florets
- 2 tablespoons olive oil
- ½ teaspoon garlic powder
- ¼ teaspoon sea salt
- ¼ teaspoon paprika
- ⅛ teaspoon ground black pepper

Instructions

Heat an air fryer to 400 degrees F (200 degrees C) following the manufacturer's instructions.

Place broccoli florets in a large, microwave-safe bowl. Cook in the microwave on high power for 3 minutes. Drain any accumulated li□uid.

Add cauliflower, olive oil, garlic powder, sea salt, paprika, and black pepper to the bowl with the broccoli. Mix well to combine. Pour mixture into the air fryer basket. Cook for 12 minutes, tossing vegetables halfway through cooking time for even browning.

Nutrition Facts

Calories: 68; Protein 2.3g; Carbohydrates 5.8g; Fat 4.7g; Sodium 103.1mg.

Air Fryer Tender Juicy Smoked BBQ Ribs

Prep time: 35 mins

Cook time: 30 mins

Total time: 1 hour 5 mins

Ingredients

- 1 rack ribs (baby back or spare ribs)
- 1 tablespoon liquid smoke
- 2-3 tablespoons pork rub I used Kansas City Gate's classic BBQ rub or McCormick's Grill Mates Pork Rub is another option
- salt and pepper to taste

- 1/2 cup BBQ sauce

Instructions

Remove the membrane from the back of the ribs.This is a thin layer that can be tough to remove. Sometimes it will peel right off. You can also cut it, and pull it off. Cut the ribs in half or so the ribs are able to fit in the air fryer.

Drizzle the liquid smoke over both sides of the ribs.

Season both sides with the pork rub, salt and pepper.

Cover the ribs and allow the ribs to sit at room temperature for 30 minutes. Add the ribs to the air fryer. It is ok to stack the ribs.

Cook for 15 minutes on 360 degrees.

Open the air fryer. Flip the ribs. Cook for an additional 15 minutes. Remove the ribs from the air fryer. Drizzle the ribs with BBQ sauce.

Nutrition Information

Calories 375, Total Fat,27g, Carbohydrates ,12 net g Protein 18g

Air-Fried Popcorn Chicken Gizzards

Prep Time: 10 mins

Cook Time: 45 mins

Additional Time: 5 mins

Total Time: 1 hr

Ingredients

- 1 pound chicken gizzards
- ⅓ cup all-purpose flour
- 1 ½ teaspoon seasoned salt
- ½ teaspoon ground black pepper
- ½ teaspoon garlic powder
- ½ teaspoon paprika
- 1 pinch cayenne pepper (optional)
- 1 large egg, beaten
- Cooking spray

Instructions

Bring a large pot of water to a boil. Cut gizzards into bite-sized pieces and add to the boiling water. Boil for 30 minutes. Drain.

Combine flour, seasoned salt, pepper, garlic powder, paprika, and cayenne in a flat plastic container. Snap the lid on and shake until combined.

Add gizzards to the seasoned flour. Snap the lid back on and shake until evenly coated.

Place beaten egg in a separate bowl. Dip each gizzard piece into the beaten egg and then place it back in the seasoned flour. Snap the lid on and shake one last time. Let sit for 5 minutes while the air fryer preheats.

Preheat the air fryer to 400 degrees F (200 degrees C).

Place gizzards in the basket and spray the tops with cooking spray. Cook for 4 minutes. Shake the basket and spray any chalky spots with more cooking spray. Cook for 4 minutes more.

Nutrition Facts

Calories: 237; Protein 23.6g; Carbohydrates 11.8g; Fat 10g; Cholesterol 330.8mg; Sodium 434.2mg

Air Fryer Crab Rangoon

Prep Time: 15 mins

Cook Time: 20 mins

Total Time: 35 mins

Ingredients

- 1 (8 ounces) package cream cheese, softened
- 4 ounces lump crab meat
- 2 tablespoons chopped scallions
- 1 teaspoon soy sauce
- 1 teaspoon Worcestershire sauce
- 1 serving nonstick cooking spray
- 24 each wonton wrappers
- 2 tablespoons Asian sweet chili sauce, for dipping

Instructions

Combine cream cheese, crab meat, scallions, soy sauce, and Worcestershire sauce in a bowl; stir until evenly combined.

Preheat an air fryer to 350 degrees F (175 degrees C). Spray the basket of the air fryer with cooking spray. Fill a small bowl with warm water.

Place 12 wonton wrappers on a clean work surface. Spoon 1 teaspoon of cream cheese mixture into the center of each wonton wrapper. Dip index finger into the warm water and wet around the sides of each wonton wrapper. Crimp wrapper corners upwards to meet in the center to form dumplings.

Place dumplings in the prepared basket and spray the tops with cooking spray.

Cook dumplings until desired crispness, about 8 to 10 minutes. Transfer to a paper towel-lined plate. While the first batch is cooking, assemble the remaining dumplings with the remaining wrappers and filling.

Serve with sweet chili sauce for dipping.

Nutrition Facts

Calories: 127; Protein 5.1g; Carbohydrates 11.1g; Fat 6.9g; Cholesterol 29.1mg; Sodium 240.4mg.

Air Fryer Cauliflower Fried Rice

Prep Time: 5 mins

Cook Time: 10 mins

Total Time: 15 mins

Ingredients

- 1 (12 ounces) package frozen cauliflower rice
- 2 large eggs
- 2 slices deli ham
- ¼ cup chopped green onions
- 2 tablespoons soy sauce

Instructions

Cook cauliflower rice in the microwave for 5 to 6 minutes. Let stand for 1 minute before carefully opening the bag.

Preheat the air fryer to 400 degrees F (200 degrees C). Cover the bottom and 1/2 inch of the basket sides with aluminum foil.

Mix cauliflower rice, eggs, ham, green onions, and soy sauce in a bowl until well combined.

Air fry for 5 minutes. Remove the basket and stir the cauliflower mixture. Return to air fryer and cook for an additional 5 minutes.

Nutrition Facts

Calories: 170; Protein 16.2g; Carbohydrates 11.6g; Fat 7.4g; Cholesterol 202mg; Sodium 1379mg.

Air Fryer Wiener Schnitzel

Prep Time: 10 mins

Cook Time: 20 mins

Total Time: 30 mins

Ingredients

- 1 pound veal, scallopini cut
- 2 tablespoons lemon juice
- salt and ground black pepper to taste
- ¼ cup all-purpose flour
- 1 egg
- 1 tablespoon chopped fresh parsley
- 1 cup panko bread crumbs nonstick cooking spray
- 1 lemon, cut into wedges

Instructions

Preheat an air fryer to 400 degrees F (200 degrees C).

Place veal on a clean work surface and sprinkle with lemon juice, salt, and pepper.

Place flour in a flat dish. Beat egg and parsley together in a second dish. Place bread crumbs in a third dish. Dredge each veal cutlet first in flour, then in the egg-parsley mixture, followed by bread crumbs, pressing down so that bread crumbs adhere.

Spray the basket of the air fryer with nonstick cooking spray. Place breaded veal cutlets into the basket, making sure not to overcrowd. Spray the tops with nonstick cooking spray.

Cook for 5 minutes. Flip, spray any chalky spots with nonstick cooking spray and cook for 5 minutes longer. Repeat with remaining veal. Serve with lemon wedges.

Nutrition Facts

Calories: 215; Protein 18g; Carbohydrates 28.4g; Fat 6.6g; Cholesterol 104.4mg; Sodium 239.3mg.

Keto Low Carb Chicken Wings

Prep Time10 mins

Cook Time20 mins

Total Time30 mins

Ingredients

- 2 pounds chicken wings I use drummettes/party wings.
- 2-3 teaspoons Chicken Seasoning or BBQ Seasoning or rub See notes for what I use.
- salt and pepper to taste
- 1 tablespoon baking powder
- 1/2 cup BBQ sauce I use sugar-free.
- 1/4 cup ChocZero Maple Syrup

Instructions

Baked Wings

Preheat oven to 375 degrees.

Season the chicken wings with the rub, salt, and pepper to taste.

Sprinkle the baking powder throughout and ensure the chicken is fully coated. Line a sheet pan with parchment paper and add the wings to the pan.

Bake for 20 minutes and then flip the wings. Bake for an additional 15-20 minutes.

Mix the maple syrup and bbq sauce together in a bowl or mixing cup.

Remove the chicken and place it in a large bowl. Drizzle the maple bbq sauce throughout.

Place the coated chicken back onto the sheet pan and bake for an additional 5 minutes. Ensure the chicken has reached an internal temperature of 165 degrees. Use a meat thermometer.

Air Fryer Wings

Season the chicken wings with the rub, salt, and pepper to taste.

Sprinkle the baking powder throughout and ensure the chicken is fully coated. Spray the air fryer basket with cooking oil. I like to use olive oil.

Add the chicken to the basket. Spray both sides with cooking oil. The white exterior on the chicken should go away when you spray it with oil.

Cook for 10 minutes on 320 degrees. Do not overcrowd the air fryer basket. Cook in batches if needed. Open the air fryer and flip the chicken. Cook for an additional 5 minutes on 400 degrees.

Mix the maple syrup and bbq sauce together in a bowl or mixing cup.

Remove the chicken and place it in a large bowl. Drizzle the maple bbq sauce throughout.

Place the chicken back in the air fryer. Cook for an additional 5 minutes on 400 degrees. Every air fryer brand is different and cook time will vary. Use your judgment. Cook until the maple bbq sauce has dried and crisped. Ensure the chicken has reached an internal temperature of 165 degrees. Use a meat thermometer.

Nutrition Facts

Calories: 424; Protein 33.4g; Sodium 1540.8mg.

Air Fryer Steak And Cheese Melts

Prep Time: 10 mins

Cook Time: 25 mins

Additional Time: 4 hrs 30 mins

Total Time: 5 hrs 5 mins

Ingredient

- 1 pound beef rib-eye steak, thinly sliced
- 2 tablespoons Worcestershire sauce
- 1 tablespoon reduced-sodium soy sauce
- 1 medium onion, sliced into petals
- 4 ounces sliced baby portobello mushrooms
- ½ green bell pepper, thinly sliced
- 1 tablespoon olive oil
- ½ teaspoon salt
- ½ teaspoon ground mustard
- ¼ teaspoon ground black pepper
- 4 hoagie rolls
- 4 slices Provolone cheese

Instructions

Place steak in a bowl and add Worcestershire and soy sauce. Cover and refrigerate 4 hours to overnight. Remove from the refrigerator and let come to room temperature, about 30 minutes.

Preheat the air fryer to 380 degrees F (190 degrees C).

Combine onion, mushrooms, and bell pepper in a large bowl. Add olive oil, salt, ground mustard, and pepper; stir to coat.

Place hoagie rolls in the basket of the air fryer and cook until toasted, about 2 minutes. Transfer rolls to a plate.

Place steak in the basket of the air fryer and cook for 3 minutes. Stir and cook for 1 more minute. Transfer to a plate.

Add vegetable mix to the basket of the air fryer and cook for 5 minutes. Stir and cook until softened, about 5 more minutes.

Stir steak into the vegetable mixture. Place cheese slices on top, slightly overlapping. Cook until cheese is melted and bubbly, about 3 minutes. Spoon mixture onto toasted rolls and serve immediately.

Nutrition Facts

Calories: 679; Protein 33.4g; Carbohydrates 75.4g; Fat 26.4g; Cholesterol 81.9mg; Sodium 1540.8mg.

Air Fryer Salmon For One

Prep Time: 5 mins

Cook Time: 15 mins

Total Time: 20 mins

Ingredient

- 1 (6 ounces) salmon fillet
- ½ teaspoon salt
- ½ teaspoon Greek seasoning (such as Cavender's®)
- ¼ teaspoon ground black pepper
- 1 pinch dried dill weed

Instructions

Preheat the air fryer to 370 degrees F (190 degrees C) for 5 minutes. Meanwhile, season salmon fillet with salt, Greek seasoning, pepper, and dill.

Line the inner basket of the air fryer with a perforated parchment round. Place salmon onto the parchment, skin side down.

Air fry salmon until salmon is cooked through, about 15 minutes.

Nutrition Facts

Calories: 189; Protein 31.1g; Carbohydrates 1.5g; Fat 5.8g; Cholesterol 72mg; Sodium 1478mg.

Easy Air Fryer French Toast Sticks

Prep Time: 10 mins

Cook Time: 10 mins

Total Time: 20 mins

Ingredient

- 4 slices of slightly stale thick bread, such as Texas toast Parchment paper
- 2 eggs, lightly beaten
- ¼ cup milk
- 1 teaspoon vanilla extract
- 1 teaspoon cinnamon
- 1 pinch ground nutmeg (optional)

Instructions

Cut each slice of bread into thirds to make sticks. Cut a piece of parchment paper to fit the bottom of the air fryer basket.

Preheat air fryer to 360 degrees F (180 degrees C).

Stir together eggs, milk, vanilla extract, cinnamon, and nutmeg in a bowl until well combined. Dip each piece of bread into the egg mixture, making sure each piece is well submerged. Shake each breadstick to remove excess liquid and place it in a single layer in the air fryer basket. Cook in batches, if necessary, to avoid overcrowding the fryer.

Cook for 5 minutes, turn bread pieces and cook for an additional 5 minutes.

Nutrition Facts

Calories: 232; Protein 11.2g; Carbohydrates 28.6g; Fat 7.4g; Cholesterol 188.4mg; Sodium 423.4mg.

Air Fryer Fish Sticks

Prep Time: 10 mins

Cook Time: 10 mins

Total Time: 20 mins

Ingredient

- 1 pound cod fillets
- ¼ cup all-purpose flour
- 1 egg
- ½ cup panko bread crumbs
- ¼ cup grated parmesan cheese
- 1 tablespoon parsley flakes
- 1 teaspoon paprika
- ½ teaspoon black pepper Cooking spray

Instructions

Preheat an air fryer to 400 degrees F (200 degrees C).

Pat fish dry with paper towels and cut into 1x3-inch sticks.

Place flour in a shallow dish. Beat egg in a separate shallow dish. Combine panko, Parmesan cheese, parsley, paprika, and pepper in a third shallow dish.

Coat each fish stick in flour, then dip in beaten egg, and finally coat in seasoned panko mixture.

Spray the basket of the air fryer with nonstick cooking spray. Arrange 1/2 the sticks in the basket, making sure none are touching. Spray the top of each stick with cooking spray.

Cook in the preheated air fryer for 5 minutes. Flip fish sticks and cook for an additional 5 minutes. Repeat with remaining fish sticks.

Nutrition Facts

Calories: 200; Protein 26.3g; Carbohydrates 16.5g; Fat 4.1g; Cholesterol 92.5mg; Sodium 245mg.

Air Fryer Keto Chicken Wings

Prep Time: 5 mins

Cook Time: 15 mins

Total Time: 20 mins

Ingredient

- 3 pounds chicken wings
- 1 tablespoon taco seasoning mix
- 2 teaspoons olive oil

Instructions

Combine chicken wings, taco seasoning, and oil in a resealable plastic bag. Shake to coat. Preheat the air fryer to 350 degrees F (175 degrees C) for 2 minutes.

Place wings in the air fryer and cook for 12 minutes, turning after 6 minutes. Serve immediately.

Nutrition Facts

Calories: 220; Protein 18.3g; Carbohydrates 1.2g; Fat 15.1g; Cholesterol 57.1mg; Sodium 187mg.

Sexy Air-Fried Meatloaf

Prep Time: 10 mins

Cook Time: 45 mins

Additional Time: 1 day

Total Time: 1 day

Ingredient

- ½ pound ground pork
- ½ pound ground veal
- 1 large egg
- ¼ cup chopped fresh cilantro
- ¼ cup gluten-free bread crumbs
- 2 medium spring onions, diced
- ½ teaspoon ground black pepper
- ½ teaspoon Sriracha salt
- ½ cup ketchup
- 2 teaspoons gluten-free chipotle chili sauce
- 1 teaspoon olive oil
- 1 teaspoon blackstrap molasses

Instructions

Preheat the air fryer to 400 degrees F (200 degrees C).

Combine pork and veal in a nonstick baking dish that fits inside the air fryer basket. Make a well and add egg, cilantro, bread crumbs, spring onions, black pepper, and 1/2 teaspoon of Sriracha salt. Mix well using your hands. Form a loaf inside the baking dish.

Combine ketchup, chipotle chili sauce, olive oil, and molasses in a small bowl and whisk well. Set aside, but do not refrigerate.

Cook meatloaf in the air fryer for 25 minutes without opening the basket. Remove meatloaf and top with ketchup mixture, covering the top completely. Return meatloaf to air fryer and bake until internal temperature reaches 160 degrees F (71 degrees C), about 7 minutes more.

Turn off the air fryer and let the meatloaf rest inside for 5 minutes. Take the meatloaf out and let rest 5 minutes more before slicing and serving.

Nutrition Facts

Calories: 272; Protein 22.1g; Carbohydrates 13.3g; Fat 14.4g; Cholesterol 123.5mg; Sodium 536.1mg.

Air-Fried Crumbed Fish

Prep Time: 10 mins

Cook Time: 12 mins

Total Time: 22 mins

Ingredient

- 1 cup dry bread crumbs
- ¼ cup vegetable oil
- 4 flounder fillets
- 1 egg, beaten
- 1 lemon, sliced

Instructions

Preheat an air fryer to 350 degrees F (180 degrees C).

Mix bread crumbs and oil in a bowl. Stir until the mixture becomes loose and crumbly.

Dip fish fillets into the egg; shake off any excess. Dip fillets into the bread crumb mixture; coat evenly and fully.

Lay coated fillets gently in the preheated air fryer. Cook until fish flakes easily with a fork, about 12 minutes. Garnish with lemon slices.

Nutrition Facts

Calories: 354; Protein 26.9g; Carbohydrates 22.5g; Fat 17.7g; Cholesterol 106.7mg; Sodium 308.9mg

Air Fryer Ranch Pork Chops

Prep Time: 5 mins

Cook Time: 10 mins

Additional Time: 10 mins

Total Time: 25 mins

Ingredient

- 4 boneless, center-cut pork chops, 1-inch thick
- cooking spray
- 2 teaspoons dry ranch salad dressing mix
- Aluminum foil

Instructions

Place pork chops on a plate and lightly spray both sides with cooking spray. Sprinkle both sides with ranch seasoning mix and let sit at room temperature for 10 minutes.

Spray the basket of an air fryer with cooking spray and preheat the air fryer to 390 degrees F (200 degrees C).

Place chops in the preheated air fryer, working in batches if necessary, to ensure the fryer is not overcrowded.

Cook for 5 minutes. Flip chops and cook 5 minutes more. Let rest on a foil-covered plate for 5 minutes before serving.

Nutrition Facts

Calories: 260; Protein 40.8g; Carbohydrates 0.6g; Fat 9.1g; Cholesterol 106.6mg; Sodium 148.2mg.

Air Fryer Frozen Chicken Wings (No Thaw)

Cook Time25 mins

Total Time25 mins

Ingredients

- 1 pound frozen chicken wings Drums and flats
- Chicken rub to taste
- Salt and pepper to taste

Instructions

Place the frozen wings in the air fryer basket. Air fry for 6 minutes on 400 degrees.

Open the air fryer basket and use a wooden spoon or spatula to break apart the chicken. You may need to air fry it for a few additional minutes if 6 minutes isn't long enough for you.

Air fry the wings for an additional 4 minutes on 400 degrees. Open the basket and season both sides of the wings.

Air fry on 400 degrees for 8 minutes. Open the basket and flip the wings.

Air fry for an additional 5 minutes on 400 degrees or until the wings have reached your desired level of crispiness, and an internal temperature of 165 degrees. The amount of wings you use and the air fryer brand and model you use may alter the cooking time. If you use more wings, allow a longer cooking time and check in on the wings to monitor doneness.

Nutrition Facts

Calories: 254; Protein 26.9g; Carbohydrates 22.5g; Fat 17.7g;

Air Fryer Rib-Eye Steak

Prep Time: 5 mins

Cook Time: 15 mins

Additional Time: 2 hrs 5 mins

Total Time: 2 hrs 25 mins

Ingredient

- 2 rib-eye steaks, cut 1 1/2- inch thick
- 4 teaspoons grill seasoning (such as Montreal Steak Seasoning®)
- ¼ cup olive oil
- ½ cup reduced-sodium soy sauce

Instructions

Combine steaks, soy sauce, olive oil, and seasoning in a large resealable bag. Marinate meat for at least 2 hours.

Remove steaks from bag and discard the marinade. Pat excess oil off the steaks.

Add about 1 tablespoon water to the bottom of the air fryer pan to prevent it from smoking during the cooking process.

Preheat the air fryer to 400 degrees F (200 degrees C).

Add steaks to air fryer and cook for 7 minutes. Turn steaks and cook for another 7 minutes until steak is medium-rare. For a medium steak, increase the total cook time to 16 minutes, flipping steak after 8 minutes.

Remove steaks, keep warm, and let sit for about 4 minutes before serving.

Nutrition Facts

Calories: 652; Protein 44g; Carbohydrates 7.5g; Fat 49.1g; Cholesterol 164.8mg; Sodium 4043.7mg.

Air-Fried Sesame-Crusted Cod With Snap Peas

Prep Time: 10 mins

Cook Time: 20 mins

Total Time: 30 mins

Ingredient

- 4 (5 ounces) cod fillets
- salt and ground black pepper to taste
- 3 tablespoons butter, melted
- 2 tablespoons sesame seeds Vegetable oil
- 2 (6 ounce) packages sugar snap peas
- 3 cloves garlic, thinly sliced
- 1 medium orange, cut into wedges

Instructions

Brush the air fryer basket with vegetable oil and preheat to 400 degrees F (200 degrees C). Thaw fish if frozen; blot dry with paper towels, and sprinkle lightly with salt and pepper.

Stir together butter and sesame seeds in a small bowl. Set aside 2 tablespoons of the butter mixture for the fish. Toss peas and garlic with the remaining butter mixture and place in the air fryer basket.

Cook peas in the preheated air fryer in batches, if needed, until just tender, tossing once, about 10 minutes. Remove and keep warm while cooking fish.

Brush fish with 1/2 of the remaining butter mixture. Place fillets in an air fryer basket. Cook 4 minutes; turn fish. Brush with the remaining butter mixture. Cook 5 to 6 minutes more or until fish begins to flake when tested with a fork. Serve with snap peas and orange wedges.

Nutrition Facts

Calories: 364; Protein 31.4g; Carbohydrates 22.9g; Fat 15.2g; Cholesterol 74.8mg; Sodium 201.5mg.

Breaded Air Fryer Pork Chops

Prep Time: 10 mins

Cook Time: 10 mins

Total Time: 20 mins

Ingredient

- 4 boneless, center-cut pork chops, 1-inch thick
- 1 teaspoon cajun seasoning
- 1 ½ cups cheese and garlic-flavored croutons
- 2 eggs
- Cooking spray

Instructions

Preheat the air fryer to 390 degrees F (200 degrees C).

Place pork chops on a plate and season both sides with Cajun seasoning.

Pulse croutons in a small food processor until they have a fine consistency; transfer to a shallow dish. Lightly beat eggs in a separate shallow dish. Dip pork chops into eggs, letting excess drip off. Coat chops in crouton breading and set on a plate. Mist chops with cooking spray.

Spray basket of the air fryer with cooking spray and place chops inside, making sure to not overcrowd the fryer. You may have to do two batches depending on the size of your air fryer.

Cook for 5 minutes. Flip chops and mist again with cooking spray if there are dry or powdery areas. Cook 5 minutes more. Repeat with remaining chops.

Nutrition Facts

Calories: 394; Protein 44.7g; Carbohydrates 10g; Fat 18.1g; Cholesterol 218mg; Sodium 428.9mg.

Air Fryer Meatballs

Prep Time: 10 mins

Cook Time: 20 mins

Additional Time: 5 mins

Total Time: 35 mins

Servings: 16

Ingredient

- 16 ounces lean ground beef
- 4 ounces ground pork
- 1 teaspoon Italian seasoning
- ½ teaspoon salt
- 2 cloves garlic, minced
- 1 egg
- ½ cup grated Parmesan cheese
- ⅓ cup Italian seasoned bread crumbs

Instructions

Preheat the air fryer to 350 degrees F (175 degrees C).

Combine beef, pork, Italian seasoning, salt, garlic, egg, Parmesan cheese, and bread crumbs in a large bowl. Mix well until evenly combined. Form into 16 equally-sized meatballs using an ice cream scoop and place on a baking sheet.

Place 1/2 of the meatballs in the basket of the air fryer and cook for 8 minutes. Shake the basket and cook 2 minutes more. Transfer to a serving plate and let rest for 5 minutes. Repeat with remaining meatballs.

Nutrition Facts

Calories: 96; Protein 7.9g; Carbohydrates 2g; Fat 6.1g; Cholesterol 35.5mg; Sodium 170.4mg.

Basic Air Fryer Hot Dogs

Prep Time: 5 mins

Cook Time: 5 mins

Total Time: 10 mins

Servings: 4

Ingredient

- 4 hot dog buns
- 4 hot dogs

Instructions

Preheat air fryer to 390 degrees F (200 degrees C).

Place buns in the basket of the air fryer and cook for 2 minutes. Remove buns to a plate. Place hot dogs in the basket of the air fryer and cook for 3 minutes. Transfer hot dogs to buns.

Air Fryer Baked Potatoes

Prep Time: 5 mins

Cook Time: 1 hr

Total Time: 1 hr 5 mins

Servings: 2

Ingredient

- 2 large russet potatoes, scrubbed
- 1 tablespoon peanut oil
- ½ teaspoon coarse sea salt

Instructions

Preheat air fryer to 400 degrees F (200 degrees C).

Brush potatoes with peanut oil and sprinkle with salt. Place them in the air fryer basket and place the basket in the air fryer.

Cook potatoes until done, about 1 hour. Test for doneness by piercing them with a fork.

Nutrition Facts

Calories: 344; Protein 7.5g; Carbohydrates 64.5g; Fat 7.1g; Sodium 462.1mg.

Air Fryer Baked Potatoes

Prep Time: 5 mins

Cook Time: 1 hr

Total Time: 1 hr 5 mins

Servings: 2

Ingredient

- 2 large russet potatoes, scrubbed
- 1 tablespoon peanut oil
- ½ teaspoon coarse sea salt

Instructions

Preheat air fryer to 400 degrees F (200 degrees C).

Brush potatoes with peanut oil and sprinkle with salt. Place them in the air fryer basket and place the basket in the air fryer.

Cook potatoes until done, about 1 hour. Test for doneness by piercing them with a fork.

Nutrition Facts

Calories: 344; Protein 7.5g; Carbohydrates 64.5g; Fat 7.1g; Sodium 462.1mg.

Air Fryer Meatloaf

Prep Time: 10 mins

Cook Time: 25 mins

Additional Time: 10 mins

Total: 45 mins

Servings: 4

Ingredient

- 1 pound lean ground beef
- 1 egg, lightly beaten
- 3 tablespoons dry bread crumbs
- 1 small onion, finely chopped
- 1 tablespoon chopped fresh thyme
- 1 teaspoon salt
- Ground black pepper to taste
- 2 mushrooms, thickly sliced
- 1 tablespoon olive oil, or as needed

Instructions

Preheat an air fryer to 392 degrees F (200 degrees C).

Combine ground beef, egg, bread crumbs, onion, thyme, salt, and pepper in a bowl. Knead and mix thoroughly. Transfer beef mixture to a baking pan and smooth the top. Press mushrooms into the top and coat with olive oil. Place the pan into the air fryer basket and slide it into the air fryer.

Set air fryer timer for 25 minutes and roast meatloaf until nicely browned. Let meatloaf rest at least 10 minutes before slicing into wedges and serving.

Nutrition Facts

Per Serving: 297 calories; protein 24.8g; carbohydrates 5.9g; fat 18.8g; cholesterol 125.5mg; sodium 706.5mg.

Crumbed Chicken Tenderloins (Air Fried)

Prep: 15 mins

Cook: 12 mins

Total: 27 mins

Servings: 4

Ingredient

- 1 egg
- ½ cup dry bread crumbs
- 2 tablespoons vegetable oil
- 8 chicken tenderloins

Instructions

Preheat an air fryer to 350 degrees F (175 degrees C).

Whisk egg in a small bowl.

Mix bread crumbs and oil in a second bowl until the mixture becomes loose and crumbly.

Dip each chicken tenderloin into the bowl of an egg; shake off any residual egg. Dip chicken into the crumb mixture, making sure it is evenly and fully covered. Lay chicken tenderloins into the basket of the air fryer. Cook until no longer pink in the center, about 12 minutes. An instant-read thermometer inserted into the center should read at least 165 degrees F (74 degrees C).

Nutrition Facts

Calories: 253; Protein 26.2g; Carbohydrates 9.8g; Fat 11.4g; Cholesterol 109mg; Sodium 170.7mg.

Air Fryer Chicken Taquitos

Prep Time: 15 mins

Cook Time: 20 mins

Total Time: 35 mins

Servings: 6

Ingredient

- 1 teaspoon vegetable oil
- 2 tablespoons diced onion
- 1 clove garlic, minced
- 2 tablespoons chopped green chiles (such as Ortega®)
- 2 tablespoons Mexican-style hot tomato sauce (such as El Pato®)
- 1 cup shredded rotisserie chicken
- 2 tablespoons Neufchatel cheese
- ½ cup shredded Mexican cheese blend
- 1 pinch salt and ground black pepper to taste
- 6 each corn tortillas
- 1 serving avocado oil cooking spray

Instructions

Heat oil in a skillet. Add onion and cook until soft and translucent, 3 to 5 minutes. Add garlic and cook until fragrant, about 1 minute. Add green chiles and Mexican tomato sauce; stir to combine. Add chicken, Neufchatel cheese, and Mexican cheese blend. Cook and stir until cheeses have melted and the mixture is completely warmed for about 3 minutes. Season with salt and pepper.

Heat tortillas in a skillet or directly on the grates of a gas stove until soft and pliable. Place 3 tablespoons of chicken mixture down the center of each tortilla. Fold over and roll into taquitos.

Preheat an air fryer to 400 degrees F (200 degrees C).

Place taquitos in the air fryer basket, making sure they are not touching, and mist with avocado oil. Cook in batches if necessary. Cook until golden brown and crispy, 6 to 9 minutes. Turn taquitos over, mist with avocado oil, and air fry for an additional 3 to 5 minutes.

Nutrition Facts

Calories: 174; Protein 10.3g; Carbohydrates 12.9g; Fat 9.2g; Cholesterol 32.6mg; Sodium 216.6mg.

Air Fryer Chicken Katsu With Homemade Katsu Sauce

Prep Time: 20 mins

Cook Time: 20 mins

Total Time: 40 mins

Servings: 4

Ingredients

Katsu Sauce:

- ½ cup ketchup
- 2 tablespoons soy sauce
- 1 tablespoon brown sugar
- 1 tablespoon sherry
- 2 teaspoons Worcestershire sauce
- 1 teaspoon minced garlic

Chicken:

- 1 pound boneless skinless chicken breast, sliced in half horizontally
- 1 pinch salt and ground black pepper to taste
- 2 large eggs, beaten

- 1 ½ cups panko bread crumbs
- 1 serving cooking spray

Instructions

Whisk ketchup, soy sauce, brown sugar, sherry, Worcestershire sauce, and garlic together in a bowl until sugar has dissolved. Set katsu sauce aside.

Preheat an air fryer to 350 degrees F (175 degrees C).

Meanwhile, lay chicken pieces on a clean work surface. Season with salt and pepper.

Place beaten eggs in a flat dish. Pour bread crumbs into a second flat dish. Dredge chicken pieces in egg and then in bread crumbs. Repeat by dredging the chicken in egg and then bread crumbs again, pressing down so that the bread crumbs stick to the chicken.

Place chicken pieces in the basket of the preheated air fryer. Spray the tops with nonstick cooking spray.

Air fry for 10 minutes. Flip chicken pieces over using a spatula and spray the tops with nonstick cooking spray. Cook for 8 minutes more. Transfer chicken to a cutting board and slice. Serve with katsu sauce.

Nutrition Facts

Calories: 318; Protein 32g; Carbohydrates 41.2g; Fat 6.7g; Cholesterol 157.6mg; Sodium 1164.4mg.

Air Fryer Lemon Pepper Shrimp

Prep Time: 5 mins

Cook Time: 10 mins

Total Time: 15 mins

Servings: 2

Ingredient

- 1 tablespoon olive oil
- 1 lemon, juiced
- 1 teaspoon lemon pepper
- ¼ teaspoon paprika
- ¼ teaspoon garlic powder
- 12 ounces uncooked medium shrimp, peeled and deveined
- 1 lemon, sliced

Instructions

Preheat an air fryer to 400 degrees F (200 degrees C).

Combine olive oil, lemon juice, lemon pepper, paprika, and garlic powder in a bowl. Add shrimp and toss until coated.

Place shrimp in the air fryer and cook until pink and firm, 6 to 8 minutes. Serve with lemon slices.

Nutrition Facts

Calories: 215; Protein 28.9g; Carbohydrates 12.6g; Fat 8.6g; Cholesterol 255.4mg; Sodium 528mg.

Dry-Rub Air-Fried Chicken Wings

Prep Time: 10 mins

Cook Time: 35 mins

Total Time: 45 mins

Servings: 2

Ingredient

- 1 tablespoon dark brown sugar
- 1 tablespoon sweet paprika
- ½ tablespoon kosher salt
- 1 teaspoon garlic powder
- 1 teaspoon onion powder
- 1 teaspoon poultry seasoning
- ½ teaspoon mustard powder
- ½ teaspoon freshly ground black pepper
- 8 chicken wings, or more as needed

Instructions

Preheat air fryer to 350 degrees F (175 degrees C).

Whisk together brown sugar, paprika, salt, garlic powder, onion powder, poultry seasoning, mustard powder, and pepper in a large bowl. Toss in chicken wings and rub the seasonings into them with your hands until fully coated.

Arrange wings in the basket of the preheated air fryer, standing up on their ends and leaning against each other and the wall of the basket.

Cook until wings are tender inside and golden brown and crisp on the outside, about 35 minutes. Transfer wings to a plate and serve hot.

Nutrition Facts

Calories: 318; Protein 25.9g; Carbohydrates 11.3g; Fat 18.7g; Cholesterol 77.3mg; Sodium 1519.9mg.

Air Fryer Chicken Cordon Bleu

Prep Time: 15 mins

Cook Time: 20 mins

Additional Time: 5 mins

Total Time: 40 mins

Servings: 2

Ingredient

- 2 boneless, skinless chicken breasts
- Salt and ground black pepper to taste
- 1 tablespoon dijon mustard
- 4 slices deli swiss cheese
- 4 slices of deli ham
- 2 toothpicks
- ¼ cup all-purpose flour
- 1 egg, beaten
- 1 cup panko bread crumbs
- ⅓ cup grated parmesan cheese
- Cooking spray

Instructions

Set 1 chicken breast on a cutting board. Hold a sharp knife parallel to the cutting board and along one long side of the breast; cut chicken breast almost in half, leaving breast attached at one side. Open breast so it lies flat like a book and covers with plastic wrap. Lightly pound with the flat side of a meat mallet to 1/4-inch thickness. Repeat with the remaining chicken breast.

Season each chicken breast with salt and pepper. Spread Dijon mustard on top. Place 1 slice of cheese on each breast. Top each with 2 slices of ham and 1 slice of cheese. Roll each breast up and secure it with a toothpick.

Place flour in a shallow bowl. Place egg in a second bowl. Mix panko bread crumbs and grated Parmesan in a third bowl.

Preheat an air fryer to 350 degrees F (175 degrees C).

Dip chicken first in flour, followed by the egg, and finally, roll in the bread crumb mixture. Spray chicken rolls with nonstick spray and let sit for 5 minutes while the air fryer preheats.

Place chicken in the basket of the preheated air fryer and cook for 10 minutes. Spray any chalky spots with nonstick spray again. Cook until chicken is no longer pink in the center, 8 minutes more.

Nutrition Facts

Calories: 728; Protein 63.7g; Carbohydrates 56.9g; Fat 31.6g; Cholesterol 253.4mg; Sodium 1663.5mg.

Cajun Air Fryer Salmon

Prep Time: 10 mins

Cook Time: 10 mins

Total Time: 20 mins

Servings: 2

Ingredient

- 2 (6 ounces) skin-on salmon fillets
- Cooking spray
- 1 tablespoon cajun seasoning
- 1 teaspoon brown sugar

Instructions

Preheat the air fryer to 390 degrees F (200 degrees C).

Rinse and dry salmon fillets with a paper towel. Mist fillets with cooking spray. Combine Cajun seasoning and brown sugar in a small bowl. Sprinkle onto a plate. Press the flesh sides of fillets into the seasoning mixture.

Spray the basket of the air fryer with cooking spray and place salmon fillets skin-side down. Mist salmon again lightly with cooking spray.

Cook for 8 minutes. Remove from air fryer and let rest for 2 minutes before serving.

Nutrition Facts

Calories: 327; Protein 33.7g; Carbohydrates 4g; Fat 18.5g; Cholesterol 99.1mg; Sodium 810.8mg.

Easy Air Fryer Pork Chops

Prep Time: 10 mins

Cook Time: 20 mins

Additional Time: 5 mins

Total Time: 35 mins

Servings: 4

Ingredient

- ½ cup grated Parmesan cheese
- 1 teaspoon paprika
- 1 teaspoon garlic powder
- 1 teaspoon kosher salt
- 1 teaspoon dried parsley
- ½ teaspoon ground black pepper
- 4 (5 ounces) center-cut pork chops
- 2 tablespoons extra virgin olive oil

Instructions

Preheat the air fryer to 380 degrees F (190 degrees C).

Combine Parmesan cheese, paprika, garlic powder, salt, parsley, and pepper in a flat shallow dish; mix well.

Coat each pork chop with olive oil. Dredge both sides of each chop in the Parmesan mixture and set on a plate.

Place 2 chops in the basket of the air fryer and cook for 10 minutes; flipping halfway through cook time.

Transfer to a cutting board and let rest for 5 minutes. Repeat with remaining chops.

Nutrition Facts

Calories: 305; Protein 35.3g; Carbohydrates 1.5g; Fat 16.6g; Cholesterol 90.3mg; Sodium 684.9mg

Lumpia In The Air Fryer

Prep Time: 15 mins

Cook Time: 20 mins

Total: 35 mins

Servings: 16

Ingredient

- 1 pound Italian hot sausage links
- ½ cup finely sliced green onions
- ¼ cup diced onions
- ½ cup finely chopped carrots
- ½ cup finely chopped water chestnuts
- 2 cloves garlic, minced
- 2 tablespoons soy sauce
- ½ teaspoon salt
- ¼ teaspoon ground ginger
- 16 spring roll wrappers
- Avocado oil
- cooking spray

Instructions

Remove casing from sausage and cook in a skillet over medium heat until slightly browned 4 to 5 minutes. Add green onions, onions, carrots, and water chestnuts. Cook and stir until onions are soft and translucent, 5 to 7 minutes. Add garlic and cook for 1 to 2 minutes. Season with soy sauce, salt, and ginger. Stir until filling is well combined and remove from heat.

Lay a spring roll wrapper at an angle. Place a scant 1/4 cup filling in the center of the wrapper. Fold bottom corner over filling and tuck in the sides to form a roll. Use your finger to lightly moisten edges with water. Repeat with remaining wrappers and filling. Mist each roll with avocado oil spray.

Preheat an air fryer to 390 degrees F (198 degrees C). Place lumpia rolls in the basket, making sure they are not touching; cook in batches if necessary. Fry for 4 minutes; flip and cook until skins are crispy, about 4 minutes more.

Nutrition Facts

Calories: 98; Protein 4.8g; Carbohydrates 7.2g; Fat 5.5g; Cholesterol 11.9mg; Sodium 471.1mg.

Air Fryer Buttermilk Fried Chicken

Prep Time: 5 mins

Cook Time: 30 mins

Additional Time: 4 hrs

Total Time: 4 hrs 35 mins

Servings: 6

Ingredient

- 1 ½ pound boneless, skinless chicken thighs
- 2 cups buttermilk
- 1 cup all-purpose flour
- 1 tablespoon seasoned salt
- ½ tablespoon ground black pepper
- 1 cup panko bread crumbs
- 1 serving cooking spray

Instructions

Place chicken thighs in a shallow casserole dish. Pour buttermilk over chicken and refrigerate for 4 hours, or overnight.

Preheat an air fryer to 380 degrees F (190 degrees C).

Mix flour, seasoned salt, and pepper in a large gallon-sized resealable bag. Dredge chicken thighs in seasoned flour. Dip back into the buttermilk, then coat with panko bread crumbs.

Spray the basket of the air fryer with nonstick cooking spray. Arrange 1/2 of the chicken thighs in the basket, making sure none are touching. Spray the top of each chicken thigh with cooking spray.

Cook in the preheated air fryer for 15 minutes. Flip. Spray tops of chicken again. Cook until chicken is no longer pink in the center and the juices run clear for about 10 more minutes. An instant-read thermometer inserted into the center should read at least 165 degrees F (74 degrees C). Repeat with the remaining chicken.

Nutrition Facts

Calories: 335; Protein 24.5g; Carbohydrates 33.2g; Fat 12.8g; Cholesterol 67.1mg; Sodium 687.2mg.

Air Fryer Potstickers

Prep Time: 10 mins

Cook Time: 25 mins

Total Time: 35 mins

Servings: 24

Ingredient

- ½ pound ground pork
- 1 (4 ounces) can water chestnuts, drained and chopped
- 1 (4 ounces) can shiitake mushrooms, drained and chopped
- 2 tablespoons soy sauce
- 2 tablespoons sesame oil
- 1 tablespoon Sriracha sauce
- 1 (12 ounces) package round dumpling wrappers

Instructions

Preheat an air fryer to 400 degrees F (200 degrees C).

Combine ground pork, water chestnuts, shiitake mushrooms, sesame oil, soy sauce, and Sriracha in a large skillet over medium-high heat. Cook until pork is no longer pink, about 6 minutes. Remove from heat and let sit until cool enough to handle.

Layout 8 dumpling wrappers on a clean work surface. Place a heaping teaspoonful of pork mixture in the middle of each wrapper. Pull both sides up like a taco and pinch the tops until sealed.

Cook in batches in the preheated air fryer for 3 minutes. Use tongs to flip the potstickers and cook 3 minutes more. Transfer to a paper-towel-lined plate. Repeat with remaining dumpling wrappers and filling.

Nutrition Facts

Calories: 70; Protein 2.7g; Carbohydrates 8.7g; Fat 2.6g; Cholesterol 4.7mg; Sodium 273.1mg.

Mexican-Style Air Fryer Stuffed Chicken Breasts

Prep Time: 20 mins

Cook Time: 10 mins

Total Time: 30 mins

Servings: 2

Ingredients

- 4 extra-long toothpicks
- 4 teaspoons chili powder, divided
- 4 teaspoons ground cumin, divided
- 1 skinless, boneless chicken breast
- 2 teaspoons chipotle flakes
- 2 teaspoons mexican oregano
- Salt and ground black pepper to taste
- ½ red bell pepper, sliced into thin strips
- ½ onion, sliced into thin strips
- 1 fresh jalapeno pepper, sliced into thin strips
- 2 teaspoons corn oil
- ½ lime, juiced

Instructions

Place toothpicks in a small bowl and cover with water; let them soak to keep them from burning while cooking.

Mix 2 teaspoons chili powder and 2 teaspoons cumin in a shallow dish. Preheat an air fryer to 400 degrees F (200 degrees C).

Place chicken breast on a flat work surface. Slice horizontally through the middle. Pound each half using a kitchen mallet or rolling pin until about 1/4-inch thick.

Sprinkle each breast half equally with remaining chili powder, remaining cumin, chipotle flakes, oregano, salt, and pepper. Place 1/2 the bell pepper, onion, and jalapeno in the center of 1 breast half. Roll the chicken from the tapered end upward and use 2 toothpicks to secure it. Repeat with other breast, spices, and vegetables and secure with remaining toothpicks. Roll each roll-up in the chili- cumin mixture in the shallow dish while drizzling with olive oil until evenly covered.

Place roll-ups in the air-fryer basket with the toothpick side facing up. Set timer for 6 minutes.

Turn roll-ups over. Continue cooking in the air fryer until juices run clear and an instant-read thermometer inserted into the center reads at least 165 degrees F (74 degrees C), about 5 minutes more. Drizzle lime juice evenly on roll-ups before serving.

Nutrition Facts

Calories: 185; Protein 14.8g; Carbohydrates 15.2g; Fat 8.5g; Cholesterol 32.3mg; Sodium 170.8mg.

Air Fryer Chimichangas

Prep Time: 15 mins

Cook Time: 20 mins

Total Time: 35 mins

Servings: 6

Ingredient

- 1 tablespoon vegetable oil
- ½ cup diced onion
- 2 cups shredded cooked chicken
- ½ (8 ounces) package Neufchatel cheese, softened
- 1 (4 ounces) can hot fire-roasted diced green chiles (such as Ortega®)

- ¼ cup chicken broth
- 1 ½ tablespoons chicken taco seasoning mix (such as McCormick®)
- ½ teaspoon salt
- ¼ teaspoon ground black pepper 6 (10 inches)
- flour tortillas
- 1 cup shredded Mexican cheese blend, or to taste
- Avocado oil
- cooking spray

Instructions

Heat oil in a medium skillet. Add onion and cook until soft and translucent, 4 to 6 minutes. Add chicken, Neufchatel cheese, diced chiles, chicken broth, taco seasoning, salt, and pepper. Cook and stir until mixture is well combined and Neufchatel has softened been incorporated.

Heat tortillas in a large skillet or directly on the grates of a gas stove until soft and pliable. Place 1/3 cup chicken mixture down the center of each tortilla and top with a heaping tablespoon of Mexican cheese. Fold top and bottom of tortillas over the filling, then roll each into a burrito shape. Mist with cooking spray and place in the basket of an air fryer.

Air fry at 400 degrees F (200 degrees C) for 4 to 6 minutes. Flip each chimichanga over, mist with cooking spray, and air fry until lightly browned, 2 to 4 minutes more.

Nutrition Facts

Calories: 455; Protein 24.8g; Carbohydrates 41g; Fat 20.6g; Cholesterol 69.8mg; Sodium 1291.5mg.

Breaded Air Fryer Pork Chops

Prep Time: 10 mins

Cook Time: 10 mins

Total Time: 20 mins

Servings: 4

Ingredient

- 4 boneless, center-cut pork chops, 1-inch thick
- 1 teaspoon Cajun seasoning
- 1 ½ cups cheese and garlic-flavored croutons
- 2 eggs

Instructions

Preheat the air fryer to 390 degrees F (200 degrees C).

Place pork chops on a plate and season both sides with Cajun seasoning.

Pulse croutons in a small food processor until they have a fine consistency; transfer to a shallow dish. Lightly beat eggs in a separate shallow dish. Dip pork chops into eggs, letting excess drip off. Coat chops in crouton breading and set on a plate. Mist chops with cooking spray.

Spray basket of the air fryer with cooking spray and place chops inside, making sure to not overcrowd the fryer. You may have to do two batches depending on the size of your air fryer.

Cook for 5 minutes. Flip chops and mist again with cooking spray if there are dry or powdery areas. Cook 5 minutes more. Repeat with remaining chops.

Nutrition Facts

Calories: 394; Protein 44.7g; Carbohydrates 10g; Fat 18.1g; Cholesterol 218mg; Sodium 428.9mg.

Air Fryer Crab Rangoon

Prep Time: 15 mins

Cook Time: 20 mins

Total Time: 35 mins

Servings: 12

Ingredient

- 1 (8 ounces) package cream cheese, softened
- 4 ounces lump crab meat
- 2 tablespoons chopped scallions
- 1 teaspoon soy sauce
- 1 teaspoon Worcestershire sauce
- 1 serving nonstick cooking spray
- 24 each wonton wrappers
- 2 tablespoons Asian sweet chili sauce, for dipping

Instructions

Combine cream cheese, crab meat, scallions, soy sauce, and Worcestershire sauce in a bowl; stir until evenly combined.

Preheat an air fryer to 350 degrees F (175 degrees C). Spray the basket of the air fryer with cooking spray. Fill a small bowl with warm water.

Place 12 wonton wrappers on a clean work surface. Spoon 1 teaspoon of cream cheese mixture into the center of each wonton wrapper. Dip index finger into the warm water and wet around the sides of each wonton wrapper. Crimp wrapper corners upwards to meet in the center to form dumplings.

Place dumplings in the prepared basket and spray the tops with cooking spray.

Cook dumplings until desired crispness, about 8 to 10 minutes. Transfer to a paper towel-lined plate. While the first batch is cooking, assemble the remaining dumplings with the remaining wrappers and filling.

Serve with sweet chili sauce for dipping.

Nutrition Facts

Calories:234; Protein 5.1g; Carbohydrates 11.1g; Fat 6.9g; Cholesterol 29.1mg; Sodium 240.4mg.

Lemon-Garlic Air Fryer Salmon

Prep Time: 10 mins

Cook Time: 10 mins

Additional Time: 5 mins

Total Time: 25 mins

Ingredient

- 1 tablespoon melted butter
- ½ teaspoon minced garlic
- 2 (6 ounce) fillets center-cut salmon fillets with skin
- ¼ teaspoon lemon-pepper seasoning
- ⅛ teaspoon dried parsley
- Cooking spray
- 3 thin slices lemon, cut in half

Instructions

Preheat the air fryer to 390 degrees F (200 degrees C). Combine melted butter and minced garlic in a small bowl.

Rinse salmon fillets and dry with a paper towel. Brush with butter mixture and sprinkle with lemon- pepper seasoning and parsley.

Spray the basket of the air fryer with cooking spray. Place salmon fillets in the basket, skin-side down, and top each with 3 lemon halves.

Cook in the preheated air fryer for 8 to 10 minutes. Remove from the air fryer and let rest for 2 minutes before serving.

Nutrition Facts

Calories: 293; Protein 33.6g; Carbohydrates 1.4g; Fat 16.4g; Cholesterol 108.3mg; Sodium 174.4mg.

Air Fryer Ranch Pork Chops

Prep Time: 5 mins

Cook Time: 10 mins

Additional Time: 10 mins

Total Time: 25 mins

Ingredient

- 4 boneless, center-cut pork chops, 1-inch thick
- Cooking spray
- 2 teaspoons dry ranch salad dressing mix
- Aluminum foil

Instructions

Place pork chops on a plate and lightly spray both sides with cooking spray. Sprinkle both sides with ranch seasoning mix and let sit at room temperature for 10 minutes.

Spray the basket of an air fryer with cooking spray and preheat the air fryer to 390 degrees F (200 degrees C).

Place chops in the preheated air fryer, working in batches if necessary, to ensure the fryer is not overcrowded.

Cook for 5 minutes. Flip chops and cook 5 minutes more. Let rest on a foil-covered plate for 5 minutes before serving.

Nutrition Facts

Calories: 260; Protein 40.8g; Carbohydrates 0.6g; Fat 9.1g; Cholesterol 106.6mg; Sodium 148.2mg.

Air Fryer Tacos De Papa

Cook Time: 25 mins

Additional Time: 5 mins

Total Time: 30 mins

Ingredient

- 2 cups water
- 1 (4 ounces) package instant mashed potatoes
- ½ cup shredded cheddar cheese
- 1 green onion, chopped
- ½ teaspoon ground cumin
- 10 corn tortillas
- 1 serving nonstick cooking spray
- ½ cup salsa verde
- ¼ cup crumbled cotija cheese

Instructions

Heat water in a medium saucepan to boiling. Remove from the heat and stir in instant mashed potatoes. Mix thoroughly with a fork to moisten all potatoes and let stand 5 minutes. Stir in Cheddar cheese, green onion, and cumin.

Preheat an air fryer to 400 degrees F (200 degrees C).

Wrap tortillas in a damp paper towel and microwave on high until warm, about 20 seconds.

Spread 1 tablespoon potato mixture in the center of a tortilla and fold over to make a taco. Repeat with remaining tortillas.

Working in batches, place tacos in the basket of an air fryer. Spray the tops with cooking spray and cook until crispy, about 5 minutes. Transfer to a serving platter and repeat to cook remaining tacos.

Drizzle salsa verde over tacos and top with cotija cheese.

Nutrition Facts

Calories: 137; Protein 4.6g; Carbohydrates 22g; Fat 3.7g; Cholesterol 9.4mg; Sodium 138.1mg.

CPSIA information can be obtained
at www.ICGtesting.com
Printed in the USA
BVHW041406270421
605944BV00006B/1391